Table of Contents

GW01418651

Introduction

"A man too busy to take care of his health is like a mechanic too busy to take care of his tools."

This Spanish proverb emphasises how important and significant it is for us to take care of our body and what happens when we let our body go without any meaningful, healthy habits. If we let the current food trends and busy lifestyle take control of our diet, then the consequences can be undesirable. It is in this context we need to know how to follow a healthy lifestyle which not only is concerned with diet alone but which is more of a lifestyle thing that we need to encompass for a longer time. In that context, ketogenic diet can help us.

And for this purpose, we have come out with this ketogenic diet e book. The book can help you to successfully adopt a ketogenic diet without much hustle as we have researched out for you, the top rated ketogenic recipes that you can start with. All the recipes are straightforward and basic without any complicated cooking techniques. Moreover, it comes with tips, to make it easier for you. So don't wait anymore to start on with this healthy lifestyle. Take care of your body and enjoy life to the fullest.

The ketogenic diet is a low carbohydrate diet in which the primary source of energy comes from fat. When a person adopts keto diet, the body is forced to break down fats instead of glucose.

When we take foods that are high in carbohydrates, the body chooses glucose over fat as the former is the easiest molecule that can be converted and used as a source of energy. For processing this glucose, production of insulin takes place in the body for taking the glucose around. Therefore, in high carb diets, fats are stored for further use and are usually stored.

On the other hand, in the case of ketogenic diet, when we lower the intake of carbohydrates to less than 15gm of carbs a day, this induces the body to a metabolic state called ketosis. Ketosis is a process that the body undertakes when there is a shortage of glucose and breaks down fat in the liver to create ketones as a major source of energy. So the main purpose of a ketogenic diet is to induce this metabolic state. Ketosis doesn't happen through starvation of calories but rather through starvation of glucose. When we are following a ketogenic diet, 75% of the energy should come from fat, 20% from protein and less than 5% from carbohydrates. Being in ketosis state is advantageous as it helps in weight loss while improving physical and mental performance. Numerous other benefits include curing epilepsy, prevention of cancer, reducing blood pressure, reduction in acne, etc.

A review done in 2014 by the International Journal of Environmental Research and Public Health regarding ketogenic diets states that "One of the most studied strategies in the recent years for weight loss is the ketogenic diet. Many studies have shown that this kind of nutritional approach has a solid physiological and biochemical basis and can induce effective weight loss along with improvement in several cardiovascular risk parameters". (1) Ketogenic diet helps in weight loss because of the lower levels of insulin and also because the stored fat is used for energy. According to another study undertaken by Bueno NB[1], de Melo IS, de Oliveira SL, regarding the benefit of low carb diet versus low-fat diet in weight loss, it says that "A modified ketogenic diet (what most people think of as a moderately **low-carb diet**) can be beneficial for most relatively healthy adults who are at an increased risk for metabolic syndrome, including those struggling with losing weight or controlling levels of blood sugar (glucose). Studies show that high-fat diets like the ketogenic diet also do not typically raise cholesterol and may reduce cardiovascular disease risk factors, especially in those who are obese". (2) Once the body reaches the state of ketosis, there would be a consistent weight loss until it reaches the optimal weight required for that person.

Ketogenic diet helps in reducing the intake of carbohydrates and nevertheless it also helps in lowering the insulin level which in turn assists in controlling diabetics. It lessens the level of insulin produced after food consumption. This is good news for those suffering from Type 2 Diabetics. It also has been noted that ketogenic diet helps in treating epilepsy and also Alzheimer's and cancer.

(1) https://www.ncbi.nlm.nih.gov/pmc/articles/PMC3945587/

(2) https://www.ncbi.nlm.nih.gov/pubmed/23651522/

PRECAUTIONS THAT NEEDED TO BE TAKEN

During the initial days of adopting ketogenic diet, you might feel tired and face digestive issues like constipation. Moreover, for certain people, they may experience keto flu. All these come up because the body is getting used to and is coping using fat as energy rather than carbohydrates. The side effects don't last more than a week or two. Make sure to drink sufficient amount of water though.

It is always advisable to ask your family physician before adopting ketogenic diet especially if you suffer from liver or kidney diseases.

Breakfast

1. Bacon, Red Chard and Ricotta Frittata

If you are looking for a breakfast recipe that will impress your family but without you taking much effort, then this creamy frittata for you. This hearty recipe with the earthy yet slightly sweet and salty flavour is sure to start your day on a healthy note as it jam packed with nutrients.

Preparation Time: 10 Minutes

Cooking Time: 30 Minutes

Servings: 8

Ingredients:

- 6 pieces Bacon, nitrate free
- 2 tablespoon Parmesan Cheese, shredded
- ½ of 1 Onion, medium and sliced thinly
- ¾ cup Ricotta Cheese

- 1 bunch Red Chard, chopped coarsely
- 1 tablespoon Heavy Cream
- Salt and freshly grounded Pepper, to taste
- 6 Eggs, preferably medium & farm raised
- ½ teaspoon Red Chili Pepper flakes

Method of Preparation:

1) Preheat the oven to 350 °F / 175 °C.
2) Heat one teaspoon of the oil in the skillet over medium heat and fry bacon for seven minutes or until cooked. Chop into smaller pieces. Tip: Don't make it crispy.
3) Return the pan to the heat and stir in the onions and sauté for three minutes or until translucent.
4) Add the chard to the pan and cook for another four minutes.
5) Spoon in the red chilli flakes, pepper and salt and give it a good stir. Set aside.
6) Whisk egg and heavy cream in medium – sized bowl until combined.
7) Stir in the both the cheeses to the bowl gradually and mix until it is just combined. Tip: It can be a bit lumpy in consistency.
8) To the pan, add the bacon first and then pour the egg mixture and spread everything evenly.
9) Finally, bake it in the oven for 18 minutes while broiling it for the last three minutes. Tip: Broiling gives it the golden yellow colour.
10) Cool for five to ten minute and then serve.

Tip: If you don't prefer chard, you can substitute it with kale.

Nutritional Information:

- ➢ Calories: 219Kcal
- ➢ Fat: 16.9g
- ➢ Carbohydrates: 3.3g
- ➢ Proteins: 12.5g

2. Crunchy Keto Granola

This low carb, dairy free breakfast fare has a great flavour, and the contrast of the textures are perfect.

Preparation Time: 5 Minutes

Cooking Time: 15 Minutes

Servings: 4

Ingredients:

- 1 cup Almonds, sliced
- 2 tablespoon Coconut Oil, melted
- 1 cup Coconut Flakes, unsweetened
- 2 teaspoon Cinnamon
- 1 cup Walnuts, coarsely diced

- Stevia Liquid, as needed

Method of Preparation:
1) Preheat oven to 375 °F / 190 °C.
2) Place all ingredients in a large sized bowl and toss them well.
3) Transfer the mixture to a greased baking sheet lined with parchment paper.
4) Spread it out in a single layer and bake it for eight to nine minutes or until it is slightly browned in colour. Tip: It would be wise to check in frequently once or twice during the cooking time.
5) Allow it to cool and then serve or store.
6) Pair it with nut milk or yoghurt of your choice.

Tip: This recipe is versatile one and therefore you can add more ingredients like chocolate chips etc. if you prefer. In place of walnuts and almonds, you can try sunflower seeds or hemp seeds. If you need to store, store in a bag with paper towels with it.

Nutritional Information:
➢ Calories: 562Kcal
➢ Fat: 54g
➢ Carbohydrates: 6g
➢ Proteins: 14.8g

3. Raspberry Crepes

These delicious low carb crepes can add colour and flavour to your breakfast fares.

Preparation Time: 10 Minutes

Cooking Time: 25 Minutes

Servings: 2

Ingredients:

- 2 Eggs, preferably small and farm – raised
- 16 Raspberries, fresh and organic
- 2-ounce Cream Cheese

- 1 teaspoon Coconut Flour
- 1 teaspoon Stevia, liquid
- ½ teaspoon Cinnamon, grounded
- Whipped Heavy Cream, to serve, as needed

Method of Preparation:

1) Start by placing the egg beater attachments and bowl in the freezer.
2) Lightly whisk eggs, coconut flour, cinnamon, stevia and cream cheese in a blender until it is frothy and combined. Set it aside for few minutes for the bubbles to disperse.
3) Place the whipped cream in the chilled bowl and whisk until fluffy. Keep it back in the refrigerator.
4) Heat a pan over medium heat and once it becomes hot, spoon in a quarter of the egg batter into the pan and cook it for two to three minutes or until bubbles appear.
5) Then, turn over to the other side and cook for another minute or so. Transfer it to a plate.
6) Repeat the procedure until all the batter is used.
7) Finally, serve the crepe by placing one spoon of the whipped cream and raspberries inside. Roll and serve.

Tip: Instead of raspberries, you can use your favourite berries. If you don't prefer to use egg, then mix one tablespoon of flax seeds along with two and a half tablespoon of water in a bowl and set it aside for four to five minutes. This mixture can be then used in the recipe instead of using eggs.

Nutritional Information:

- ➢ Calories: 244Kcal
- ➢ Fat: 20g
- ➢ Carbohydrates: 4g
- ➢ Proteins: 9g

4. Mocha Chia Pudding

Looking for a healthy nutritious breakfast? Look no further; for here comes a highly flavourful yet nicely textured pudding that is full of Omega 3 fatty acids along with fibre and proteins.

Preparation Time: 5 Minutes

Cooking Time: 30 Minutes

Servings: 2

Ingredients:

- 2 tablespoon Herbal Coffee
- 1 tablespoon Vanilla Extract, preferably organic
- 2 tablespoon Cacao Nibs
- ⅓ cup Chia Seeds, dry
- 1 tablespoon Liquid Stevia
- ⅓ cup Coconut Cream, undiluted

Method of Preparation:

1) First, boil two cups of water with the herbal coffee in a deep pan over medium heat for about 12 to 13 minutes.
2) Once the coffee is strained, combine coconut cream, stevia and vanilla extract along with the coffee in a bowl.
3) Stir in the cacao nibs and chia seeds to the bowl and stir them well.
4) Transfer them to the serving bowls and place them in the refrigerator for about 20 to 25 minutes.
5) Sprinkle with extra cacao nibs.

Tip: Instead of herbal coffee, you can try dark chocolate or even regular coffee if you prefer.

Nutritional Information:

- ➢ Calories: 257Kcal
- ➢ Fat: 20.25g
- ➢ Carbohydrates: 2.25g
- ➢ Proteins: 7g

5. Protein Waffles

Wow your taste buds with these heavenly tasting waffles that are perfect for breakfast as well as a post workout snack.

Preparation Time: 10 Minutes

Cooking Time: Minutes

Servings: Makes 5

Ingredients:

- 1 cup Almond Flour
- 4 tablespoon Coconut Oil, melted
- 1 cup Almond Milk
- 1 cup Whey Protein

- 2 Eggs, preferably small and farm raised
- ½ teaspoon Sea Salt
- 1 tablespoon Baking powder, low sodium & low aluminium

Method of Preparation:

1) Preheat the waffle iron to high heat.
2) Combine almond flour in a medium sized bowl with baking powder, whey protein and salt until mixed.
3) Then, mix coconut oil, eggs and almond milk in another bowl.
4) Stir together the almond flour mixture into the coconut oil mixture. Set it aside for five minutes.
5) Spoon the mixture onto the waffle iron and cook according to the waffle maker instructions.
6) Serve it along with eggs.

Tip: Instead of Almond flour you can use grounded flax seeds and instead of Almond milk, you can use unflavoured hemp milk.

Nutritional Information:

- Calories: 182Kcal
- Fat: 15.6g
- Carbohydrates: 2g
- Proteins: 10.61g

6. Cauliflower Hash Browns

Cauliflower hash browns are delightful and delish in taste, and you can take them without any guilt as these hash browns are so healthy.

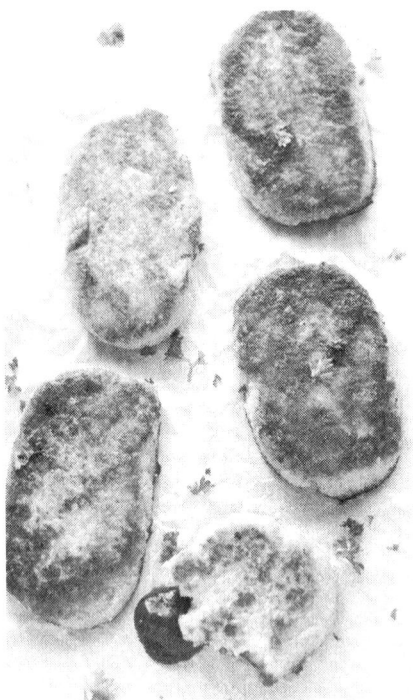

Preparation Time: 15 Minutes

Cooking Time: 30 Minutes

Servings: Makes 6

Ingredients:

- 3 Cups Cauliflower, grated
- 1/8 teaspoon Black Pepper
- 1 Egg, preferably large and farm raised
- ¼ teaspoon garlic powder
- ¾ cup Cheddar Cheese, shredded

- ¼ teaspoon Cayenne Pepper
- ½ teaspoon Sea Salt

Method of Preparation:

1) Microwave grated cauliflower in a bowl for about two to three minutes.
2) Allow it to cool and keep it on paper towels so that the water is drained from them.
3) Combine the drained cauliflower and the remaining ingredients to make a mixture.
4) Now, make balls out of this mixture and arrange the patties on a greased baking sheet lined with parchment paper.
5) Bake it at 400 °F / 200 °C for a quarter of an hour or until cooked.
6) Allow it to cool and serve it warm along with dipping sauce or with homemade mayonnaise.

Tip: Garnish with green onions for extra taste.

Nutritional Information:

- Calories: 162Kcal
- Fat: 11.25g
- Carbohydrates: 3.2g
- Proteins: 7g

7. Pork Rind Cereal

Pork rind cereals are very easy to make and have such a good combination of flavours. These cereals are a lot healthier and tastier than the sugar laden cereals.

Preparation Time: 10 Minutes

Cooking Time: 20 Minutes + 30 Minutes (Cooling Time)

Servings: 2

Ingredients:

- 1-ounce Pork Rinds
- ¼ teaspoon Cinnamon, grounded
- 1 tablespoon Erythritol
- 2 tablespoon Butter, organic
- 2 tablespoon Heavy Cream

Method of Preparation:

1) First, melt butter in a medium sized saucepan over medium heat.

2) Remove the pan from the heat and stir in heavy cream and Erythritol and mix them well.

3) Return the pan back to the heat and caramelise it until bubbles start coming.

4) Add the pork rinds to the pan and combine until the pork rinds are coated completely with the caramelised mixture.

5) Off the heat and transfer the pork rinds to an aluminium foil lined plate and cool it for some time.

6) After that, place it in the refrigerator for about 20 to 25 minutes and then serve.

7) Serve it with the milk of your choice.

Tip: If you prefer, you can garnish it with nuts. Look for pork rinds that are soft rather than hardened ones.

Nutritional Information:
- Calories: 512Kcal
- Fat: 47g
- Carbohydrates: 2.5g
- Proteins: 14g

Soup and Salads

8. Buffalo Chicken Soup

Warm up your wintry evenings with slightly spicy yet distinctively rich soup that comes with the bold flavours of buffalo chicken.

Preparation Time: 15 Minutes

Cooking Time: 3 Hour and 15 Minutes

Servings: 5

Ingredients:

- 1 ¼ ounce Chicken, boneless and sliced
- ½ teaspoon Gelatin
- 1 small onion, chopped finely
- 2-ounce Cream Cheese
- 1 cup Heavy Cream
- 2 to 3 cloves of Garlic, finely minced
- 1 tablespoon Celery tops, minced

- 3 cups Beef Broth
- 4-ounce Butter, organic
- 1/3 cup Hot Sauce
- Salt and Black Pepper, as needed

Method of Preparation:

1) Start by placing all the ingredients excluding the cream cheese and flax seeds in the crock pot at high heat for three hours or until thoroughly cooked.
2) Spoon the chicken pieces from the crockpot and transfer it to plate. Shred it.
3) Combine the gelatin with cold water and mix it well. Set it aside for five minutes.
4) Add the gelatin mixture and cream cheese to the crockpot and stir.
5) Then, with the help of an immersion blender, emulsify until it becomes it a smooth soup.
6) Return the shredded chicken pieces into the crockpot and mix everything.
7) Season the soup with salt, pepper and hot sauce as needed.
8) Serve it hot along with your choice of tangy cheese.

Tip: Instead of using gelatin, you can also use xanthum gum.

Nutritional Information:

➢ Calories: 523.2Kcal
➢ Fat: 44.2g

- ➢ Carbohydrates: 3.4g
- ➢ Proteins: 20.8g

9. Broccoli Soup

This thick and hearty soup is excellent in taste and highly satiating and will satisfy the palettes of all your loved ones.

Preparation Time: 5 Minutes

Cooking Time: 20 Minutes

Servings: 3

Ingredients:

- 1 Leek, medium and white portion, chopped
- 1 teaspoon Black Pepper
- 1 Garlic clove
- 3 ounces Butter, organic
- 2 ½ cups Chicken Broth
- 2 Broccoli head, medium and chopped into small florets
- 1 teaspoon Celtic Salt
- ½ cup Heavy Cream,
- 1 tablespoon Parsley, fresh and finely chopped

Method of Preparation:

1) Heat the butter in a medium sized skillet over low heat.

2) Stir in the garlic and leek into the pan and cook for four to five minutes or until the leek becomes translucent.

3) Next, add the broccoli and the stock; bring it to simmer over low heat for six minutes. Tip: The soup should cover the florets.

4) Once cooked, remove it from heat.

5) Using an immersion blender, blend into a smooth soup without any lumps.

6) Season with salt, pepper and parsley.

7) Serve it hot.

Tip: If you prefer you can have sliced bacon pieces into it before serving for a richer taste.

Nutritional Information:

➤ Calories: 402Kcal

➤ Fat: 38g

➤ Carbohydrates: 6g

➤ Proteins: 6g

10.   Shrimp Stacked Salad

If your tongue is ready for an explosion of flavours, then the layers of flavours in this stacked salad is sure to impress you as it has the perfect combination of sweetness, sour and spiciness.

Preparation Time: 15 Minutes

Cooking Time: 20 Minutes

Servings: 4

Ingredients:

- ½ pound of Shrimp, cooked and tails removed
- 1 Garlic clove, minced
- 4 cups Lettuce, fresh and organic
- 4 Eggs, farm raised, hard boiled and sliced
- 4 tablespoons extra-virgin Olive Oil
- 2 tablespoons Vinegar, balsamic
- 12 slices Bacon, cooked and chopped
- 1 Roma tomato, organic and finely diced

- 2 Avocado, organic and chopped
- ½ Cucumber, organic and sliced finely
- 2 tablespoon Parsley, fresh and finely chopped
- 1 teaspoon Dijon mustard
- Salt and Black Pepper, as needed

Method of Preparation:

1) To begin with, combine Dijon mustard, minced garlic, pepper and salt in a small mixing bowl.
2) Pour the vinegar first and then the olive oil gradually while whisking it continuously. Keep it aside.
3) Start stacking the salad with the help of stack ring or something similar to that.
4) First place the lettuce leaves, and then the remaining ingredients with the shrimp at the top.
5) Finally, drizzle the seasoning over the stacked salad and serve immediately.

Tip: You can even add brown rice to the mix to make it more full and satiating.

Nutritional Information:

- Calories: 545Kcal
- Fat: 51.2g
- Carbohydrates: 5.5g
- Proteins: 11.7g

11.   Grilled Portobello Caesar Salad

Here is a tasty, quick – cooking salad recipe that features thick, juicy and meaty grilled mushrooms in a brightly flavoured cheesy anchovy dressing.

Preparation Time: 20 Minutes

Cooking Time: 15 Minutes

Serving: 4

Ingredients:

- 2 Romaine Lettuce, large heads, rinsed and pat dried, torn
- 4 Portobello mushrooms, large
- 4-ounce Parmesan Cheese, shaved
- 1 tablespoon Olive Oil

- Sea Salt and Black Pepper, as needed

For the dressing:
- ¼ cup Parmesan Cheese, grated
- ½ cup Olive Oil
- 2 Anchovy filets, large
- ¼ teaspoon Pepper, freshly grounded
- 2 Egg yolks, small and farm raised
- 1 Lemon, juiced and zest
- 2 Garlic cloves, chopped coarsely
- ¼ teaspoon Sea Salt

Method of Preparation:
1) Blend parmesan cheese, garlic cloves, egg yolks and anchovy filets in a food processor for two minutes or until it becomes a thick and smooth paste.
2) To this, spoon in the lemon zest and juice along with the seasonings and blend again.
3) Gradually pour the olive oil into it until it is emulsified and well combined.
4) In the meantime, preheat the grill to medium heat.
5) Marinate the mushrooms with salt and pepper and apply oil over them.
6) Grill them with top side down for about four minutes, then flip and cook for another four minutes.
7) After that, slice them thinly and set the mushrooms aside.
8) Finally, arrange the torn lettuce leaves first, then the parmesan cheese and finally the grilled mushroom slices.

9) Drizzle the dressing and serve it immediately.

Tip: This salad pairs well with the broccoli soup.

Nutritional Information:

➢ Calories: 515Kcal

➢ Fat: 43.15g

➢ Carbohydrates: 6.5g

➢ Proteins: 16.27g

12.   Big Mac Salad

For those times when you feel like having the high carb fast food, this big mac salad is an excellent way to bring a healthy version of that to your table.

Preparation Time: 15 Minutes

Cooking Time:

Servings: 6

Ingredients:

- 1-pound Beef, grounded
- ¾ cup Cheddar Cheese, finely shredded
- 1 teaspoon Sea salt
- 1 cup Tomatoes, finely chopped
- ¼ teaspoon Black pepper, grounded
- ½ cup Pickles, diced
- 8-ounce Iceberg lettuce

To make the Dressing:

- ½ teaspoon Paprika, smoked
- ½ cup Mayonnaise
- 1 ½ tablespoon Liquid Stevia
- 2 tablespoon Pickles, diced
- 2 teaspoon Mustard
- 1 teaspoon Vinegar, white

Method of Preparation:

1) Start by marinating the beef with salt and pepper and set it aside.
2) Cook the beef in a wide skillet over medium – high heat for eight minutes or until the meat is browned.
3) In the meantime, place all the ingredients needed to make the dressing in a blender and blend until it becomes a smooth paste.
4) Place the dressing in the refrigerator until needed.
5) Mix all the remaining ingredients necessary for the salad in a large mixing bowl and toss them well.
6) Add the beef pieces and drizzle the salad dressing. Toss again.
7) Serve immediately.

Tip: For a spicier kick, you can add cayenne pepper to the dressing.

Nutritional Information:

- Calories: 368kcal

- ➢ Fat: 31g
- ➢ Carbohydrates: 2g
- ➢ Proteins: 18g

Seafood

13.   Trout with Orange sauce

The flavour combination in this recipe is fuelled by the light, fresh taste of trout and sweet, nutty flavour of the pecans.

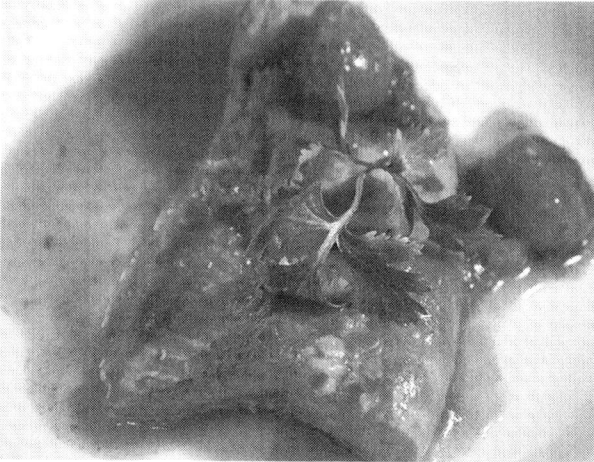

Preparation Time: 10 Minutes

Cooking Time: 20 Minutes + 1 Hour Marination Time

Serving: 2 to 3

Ingredients:

- 8-ounce Trout fillet
- ½ cup Pecans, chopped
- 1 tablespoon Olive Oil
- 1 tablespoon Butter, organic
- Salt and Black Pepper, to taste
- Juice and Zest from 1 Orange
- Fresh Parsley, for garnish

Method of Preparation:

1) Season the fish with salt and pepper and set it aside for at least half an hour or maximum of one to two hours.

2) Heat olive oil in a large pan over medium high heat and once it becomes hot, add the fish fillet.

3) Sear the fish for four minutes per side and then flip and sear the other side until the fish flakes easily and is crispy.

4) Transfer the seared fish to a paper lined plate and set it aside.

5) In the same pan, melt butter over medium heat and to this, stir in the chopped pecans.

6) After a minute or so, pour the orange juice into the pan and allow it to boil.

7) As it gets reduced, season it with salt and pepper as needed. Remove from heat.

8) Finally, drizzle the orange dressing over the trout and garnish it with the orange zest.

Tip: You can add honey also if you want a slightly sweeter taste. Instead of pecans, you can try using panko breadcrumbs also, but the taste would be different.

Nutritional Information:

➤ Calories: 369Kcal
➤ Fat: 33.09g
➤ Carbohydrates: 7.2g
➤ Proteins: 11.17g

14.   Smoked Salmon and Sprouts

Thin strips of salmon are sautéed along with subtle and delicate flavoured leeks and strongly flavoured beans sprout in this quick, simple and crowd pleasing fare.

Preparation Time: 10 Minutes

Cooking Time: 10 Minutes

Servings: 2

Ingredients:

- 2 tablespoon Coconut Oil
- 2-ounce Bean Sprouts
- 1 pound Leeks, sliced finely
- ½ cup Greek Yogurt, full - fat

- 4-ounce Salmon, smoked and sliced into thin strips
- Black Pepper, freshly grounded

Method of Preparation:

1) Heat oil in a large frying pan; cook leeks over medium heat until it becomes translucent.
2) Add the salmon and spoon in the Greek yoghurt into it and stir until just combined.
3) Cook for three to four minutes or until the fish is cooked.
4) Check for seasoning and add pepper and salt as needed.
5) Finally, stir in the sprouts and give everything a good stir.
6) Serve it along with couscous.

Tip: Instead of beans shoots, you can use any sprouts.

Nutritional Information:

- Calories: 219kcal
- Fat:18.12g
- Carbohydrates: 1.2g
- Proteins: 12.4g

15.   Srilankan Fish Curry

If you are looking for a lunch fare that is filling, but which is a bit decadent yet low carb, then this Srilankan fish curry with the exotic flavour of coconut, spices and chillies is for you.

Preparation Time: 15 Minutes

Cooking Time: 25 Minutes

Servings:4

Ingredients:

- 4 × 7ounce White Fish fillets
- ½ teaspoon Celtic Sea Salt
- 4 tablespoon Coconut Oil
- ½ teaspoon Turmeric powder
- ½ of 1Red Onion, small and chopped finely
- ½ teaspoon Mustard seeds, whole
- 2 long Green chillies, chopped

- 1 teaspoon Curry Powder
- ½ cup Water
- 1 teaspoon Ginger, grated.
- ¼ cup Cilantro, fresh and chopped
- ¼ teaspoon Cumin, grounded
- 3 cloves of garlic, chopped
- 1 ½ cup Coconut Cream, full fat

Method of Preparation:

1) First heat oil in a skillet over medium heat and stir in the mustard seeds.
2) Once the mustard seeds start popping, add the onion, ginger and garlic and cook for four minutes or until the onions become transparent and garlic becomes fragrant.
3) Spoon in the turmeric powder, curry powder, chillies and cumin into the skillet and stir.
4) Sauté it for four minutes and then pour the coconut milk into it. Stir.
5) Bring the mixture to a boil and simmer it for ten to twelve minutes.
6) In the meantime, fry the fish in a wide pan over medium heat.
7) Cook for three to four minutes per side or until the fish is cooked and crispy.
8) Finally, add the cooked fish pieces into the skillet and cook for four minutes or until everything is well incorporated.
9) Garnish it with cilantro leaves and serve it hot.
10) It pairs well with carb rice.

Tip: If you want the dish to be less spicy, then you can deseed the chillies.

Nutritional Information:
- ➢ Calories: 535Kcal
- ➢ Fat: 37g
- ➢ Carbohydrates: 4.75g
- ➢ Proteins: 44g

16.   Avocado Crab Salad

This is a great basic recipe for a weekday meal that the whole family will love. The satisfying creaminess from the avocado coalesces perfectly with the fresh and light flavour of the crab in this easy meal.

Preparation Time: 10 Minutes

Cooking Time: 15 Minutes

Servings: 2

Ingredients:

- 1 Hass Avocado, medium and halved, pit removed
- ½ teaspoon Olive Oil
- 4-ounce lump Crab Meat
- 1 tablespoon Cilantro, fresh and chopped
- 1 ½ tablespoon Lime juice, fresh
- 2 tablespoon Red Onion, chopped

- 2 grape Tomatoes, finely diced
- ¼ teaspoon Salt and Black Pepper

Method of Preparation:

1) Combine onion in a medium – sized bowl along with tomatoes, lime juice, olive oil and cilantro; season to taste.
2) Now add crab meat to it and mix them well.
3) Spoon out the avocado meat and fill in the crab salad into it.
4) Serve immediately.

Tip: Garnish with chives for extra flavour.

Nutritional Information:

➤ Calories: 178Kcal
➤ Fat: 13g
➤ Carbohydrates: 4g
➤ Proteins: 9.5g

17.   Tuna Deviled Eggs

This easy tuna appetiser that can be put together with few simple ingredients. These deviled eggs are absolutely delightful and enjoyable to gorge on with their creamy and zesty filling.

Preparation Time: 10 Minutes

Cooking Time: 15 Minutes

Servings: 4

Ingredients:

- 4 Eggs, large & farm raised, hard boiled
- 1 Spring Onion, large and sliced
- 2 tablespoon Mayonnaise
- 3-ounce Tuna, drained

- 1 tablespoon Sriracha sauce
- Sea Salt and Black Pepper, to taste

Method of Preparation

1) Halve the hard boiled eggs and spoon out the egg yolk.
2) In a medium sized mixing bowl, combine tuna, sriracha sauce, egg yolks, spring onion and mayonnaise along with salt and pepper and give everything a good stir. Tip: Reserve a small portion for garnishing.
3) Scoop in the egg tuna mixture into the egg whites.
4) Garnish with the remaining spring onion or with basil serves and serve.

Tip: Instead of tuna, you can use also use cooked chicken or sautéed mushrooms.

Nutritional Information:

➢ Calories: 151 Kcal
➢ Fat: 11.4g
➢ Carbohydrates: 1.1g
➢ Proteins: 10.7g

18.   Fish Pie

Here comes a gourmet keto twist on the classic British fish pie. The pie is fresh, healthy and has a little bit of kick. Utterly scrumptious.

Preparation Time: 10 Minutes

Cooking Time: 30 Minutes

Servings:2

Ingredients:

- 2 Pollock Fish Fillets, large
- ½ cup Heavy Cream
- 1 cup Cheddar Cheese
- 1 Cauliflower head, small and chopped into florets
- 2 tablespoon Butter, organic
- 1 Carrot, medium and sliced
- 1 cup Spinach
- ½ teaspoon Dill, chopped

- ½ teaspoon Parsley, chopped
- ½ of 1 Fish Stock cube
- ½ teaspoon white Pepper
- ¼ cup Water

Method of Preparation:

1) To start with, fry the fish in a wide skillet over medium heat until it is cooked and fish flakes easily. Transfer it to a plate lined with paper towel.
2) Place the cauliflower and carrot in a steamer for five to six minutes or until cooked and soft.
3) In the meantime, heat oil in a saucepan over medium heat and to this, stir in the spinach and cook for one to two minutes or until it is wilted.
4) Pour the stock, heavy cream, parsley, dill, pepper and salt into the pan and stir until everything is well combined.
5) Lower the heat and simmer until the sauce has reached your desired consistency.
6) Once the vegetables are cooked, transfer the cauliflower to a plate and pat it dry with a towel.
7) Add half the quantity of cheese and the cauliflower into the blender and pulse it once.
8) Stir in the carrot into the sauce and give a mix.
9) Finally, spoon in the pie filling into a pie pan and then with the cauliflower mixture and spread it out evenly.
10) Bake it in the oven until cooked and the crust has become crispy.

11) Sprinkle the remaining cheese and grill until it becomes golden yellow in colour and gooey on top.
12) Serve it hot.

Tip: If you don't prefer cheese, then you can use ghee or if not butter while making the cauliflower puree.

Nutritional Information:
➢ Calories:555Kcal
➢ Fat: 54g
➢ Carbohydrate: 7g
➢ Proteins: 34g

19.   Tandoori Salmon

A comforting salmon fare packed with rich Indian flavours comes your way through this recipe for seafood. Pair it with the refreshing, crunchy cucumber salad, and you have a highly appetising meal before you.

Preparation Time: 10 Minutes

Cooking Time: 20 Minutes

Servings: 4

Ingredients:

- 1½ pound Salmon, small pieces
- 2 tablespoon Coconut Oil
- 1 tablespoon Tandoori Seasoning

To make the Cucumber Sauce:

- 1¼ cup Sour Cream
- Juice of ½ Lime
- ½ of 1 Cucumber, shredded

- ½ teaspoon Sea Salt
- 2 cloves of Garlic, crushed

To make the Salad:
- 3½ oz. Arugula Lettuce
- 3 Scallions, chopped
- 1 Yellow Bell Pepper, chopped
- Juice of 1 Lime
- 2 Avocados, chopped

Method of Preparation:

1) Preheat the oven to 350 ° F / 175 ° C.
2) Mix tandoori seasoning and coconut oil and then apply this marinade over the salmon pieces. Set it aside for half an hour.
3) Bake the salmon for 18 to 22 minutes or until the fish flakes easily.
4) In the meantime, combine sour cream, garlic, lime juice and shredded cucumber in a small mixing bowl until mixed well. Tip: Make sure to remove all water from cucumber.
5) Toss together all the ingredients needed for salad in a big mixing bowl.
6) Place the fish fillets on top of the salad and drizzle the cucumber sauce over it.
7) Serve and enjoy.

Tip: Serve it with poppadoms for more crunchiness factor while serving.

Nutritional Information:

- ➢ Calories: 646Kcal
- ➢ Fat: 44.08g
- ➢ Carbohydrates: 8g
- ➢ Proteins: 40g

20.   Bacon Wrapped Scallops

A super quick, simple and filling bacon wrapped scallops recipe that kids and adults would love alike.

Preparation Time: 5 Minutes

Cooking Time: 10 Minutes

Servings: 4

Ingredients:

- 12 Scallops
- 1 tablespoon Coconut Oil
- Salt and Black Pepper, as needed
- 12 Bacon, sliced thinly

Method of Preparation:

1) Marinate the scallops with salt and pepper and set it aside.
2) Wrap each of the scallops with the bacon and secure it with toothpicks.

3) Heat the oil in a wide saucepan over medium heat and add the bacon wrapped scallops into it.
4) Cook each of them for two to three minutes each side or until cooked.
5) Check for taste and add more seasoning if needed.
6) Garnish with cilantro leaves, if desired.

Tip: For a complete meal, you can serve it along with lettuce leaves, avocado slices and a spicy dipping sauce.

Nutritional Information:
➢ Calories: 204Kcal
➢ Fat: 10g
➢ Carbohydrates: 3g
➢ Proteins:27g

Poultry

21.   Buffalo Chicken Strips

Would you like to be ooohed and awed over your food by your guests? Then make these zesty, spicy chicken tenders and you sure to get rave reviews for these as they are so crunchy and savoury.   Furthermore, the creamy flavour of the blue cheese dressing is simply awesome.

Preparation Time: 15 Minutes

Cooking Time: 1 Hour

Servings: 3

Ingredients:

- 5 Chicken fillets, preferably breasts
- 2 Garlic cloves, finely minced
- ¾ Cup Almond Flour
- 1 tablespoon Chilli powder
- 8 tablespoon Hot Sauce

- 1 tablespoon Paprika
- 4 tablespoon Olive Oil
- 2 Eggs, large and farm raised
- 3 tablespoon Butter, organic
- 2 teaspoon Sea Salt
- 3 tablespoon Blue Cheese
- 2 teaspoon Black Pepper
- 1 teaspoon Onion powder

Method of Preparation:

1) Preheat the oven to 400 ° F / 200 ° C.
2) Mix garlic, onion powder, paprika, pepper, chilli powder and salt in a small mixing bowl.
3) Then with the help of a meat pounder, flatten the chicken fillets into ½ inch thickness and halve them into two pieces each.
4) Marinate the chicken pieces with 1/3 rd of the spice mix each side and set it aside for quarter of an hour.
5) In the meantime, mix together almond flour and the remaining 1/3 rd of the spice mix.
6) Whisk the eggs lightly in another bowl.
7) Immerse the chicken pieces first into the egg mixture and then to the almond mixture until it is properly coated.
8) Place a foil on a baking sheet and then arrange the seasoned chicken pieces and bake them for 13 minutes.
9) Melt butter in a small saucepan over medium heat and to this, spoon in the hot sauce and mix them well. Keep it aside.

10) Once the time is over, take the baking sheet out and apply olive oil over one part of the chicken pieces and return them back to the oven for broiling it for two minutes.

11) Next, apply the oil to the other side and repeat the same procedure.

12) Allow the chicken pieces to cool and then drizzle the buffalo sauce over them if desired.

13) Serve it along with blue cheese crumbles.

Tip: If you are planning to spoon the sauce over the wings rather than dipping them, pour them while the wings are hot so that they absorb more.

Nutritional Information:

➢ Calories: 683Kcal
➢ Fat: 54g
➢ Carbohydrates: 4.8g
➢ Proteins: 41g

22.   Bell Peppers with Turkey

You will love these enticing stuffed peppers and be surprised at how well the ingredients go together. The spices and the hot sauce complement the ground turkey and the peppers perfectly well.

Preparation Time: 10 Minutes

Cooking Time: 35 Minutes

Servings: 3

Ingredients:

- 1-pound Turkey, grounded
- ½ teaspoons Nutmeg, grounded
- 3 Bell Pepper, medium, deseeded and tops removed
- 2 tablespoons Paprika

- 3 tablespoons Mozzarella Cheese, shredded
- 1 Garlic clove, minced
- 2 tablespoons Hot Sauce
- 2 teaspoons Italian Seasoning
- Sea Salt, as needed
- 2 tablespoons Olive Oil
- ½ of 1 Red Onion, chopped

Method of Preparation:

1) Preheat the oven to 350 ° F / 175 ° C.
2) Heat oil in a medium sized skillet over medium high heat.
3) Stir in the minced garlic and sauté for a minute or until aromatic.
4) Then, add the onion and cook them for two to three minutes or until cooked.
5) Add the grounded turkey and cook them for six to seven minutes or until colour changes to brown.
6) If lumps come up, spoon it down and stir in paprika, nutmeg, Italian seasonings, hot sauce and salt and give a good stir. Allow it to cool.
7) Fill the insides of the bell pepper with the meat stuffing and arrange the peppers on a baking sheet greased with oil.
8) Bake it for 25 minutes and take out the peppers.
9) Garnish it with the cheese and bake for further four minutes or until the cheese has melted.
10) Serve.

Tip: You can serve these stuffed peppers along with low carb Caprese salad.

Nutritional Information:

- ➤ Calories: 456Kcal
- ➤ Fat: 34g
- ➤ Carbohydrates: 5.8g
- ➤ Proteins: 30.6g

23.   Low Carb Lasagne

The preparation of this low carb lasagne couldn't be simpler. It packed in so much flavour but without the usual high amount of starchy carbs that you get when eating the typical carb laden lasagne.

Preparation Time: 15 Minutes

Cooking Time: 45 Minutes

Servings: 12

Ingredients:

- 14-ounce Artichoke Hearts, quartered, drained
- ½ cup Pine Nuts, chopped
- 1 cup Basil, fresh and torn
- 1-pound Chicken Breast, shaved thinly

- 1 × 24-ounce jar Marinara Sauce, low carb or homemade

To make the Sauce:
- 1 cup Chicken Stock, organic
- 4 cups Goat Cheese, hard and shredded
- 4-ounce Goat Cheese, soft
- 2 Eggs, small & farm raised

Method of Preparation:
1) First, preheat the oven to 350 ° F / 175 ° C.
2) Pour stock into a deep pan and heat it over medium heat.
3) To this, stir in the soft goat cheese first and mix it well.
4) Once it is well combined, add the hard goat cheese and stir until everything is well incorporated.
5) Gradually spoon in the egg to this mixture and give a good stir.
6) Spoon half the quantity of the marinara sauce into a wide baking dish and then layer it with shaved chicken breast, then with half the artichokes and later with the cheese sauce. Sprinkle the basil leaves and pine nuts on top.
7) Bake for half an hour or until the cheese becomes all golden yellow in coloured and gooey and cooked.
8) Allow it to cool for some time before serving.

Tip: If you prefer, you can add zucchini into strips and add along as one of the layers.

Nutritional Information:

- ➢ Calories: 305Kcal
- ➢ Fat: 15g
- ➢ Carbohydrates: 5.5g
- ➢ Proteins: 24.5g

24.   Roasted Duck with Cranberry Glaze

This recipe combines the crispy fun of roasted duck with the exotic flavour of cardamom infused cranberry orange glaze. Take one bite, and your taste buds are gonna burst out with all the flavours in it.

Preparation Time: 15 Minutes

Cooking Time: 1 Hour 30 Minutes

Servings: 3 to 4

Ingredients:

- 6-pound duck, whole
- 2 cups Water
- ½ teaspoon Xanthan gum
- 2 tablespoon Stevia
- 1 cup Cranberries, fresh

- Juice and Zest of 1 Orange
- ¼ teaspoon Orange Extract

Method of Preparation:
1) Bake the duck at 325 ° F / 160 ° C for 25 to 28 minutes.
2) Lower the heat to 300 ° F / 150 ° C for about 50 to 60 minutes.
3) Turn over the duck and with the help of a fork, pork holes onto the skin.
4) Roast the bird again for another 25 to 30 minutes.
5) In the meantime, place cranberries, orange juice, water, orange zest and cardamom in a medium sized saucepan over medium heat and bring it to boil.
6) Allow it to simmer for 18 minutes. Set it aside.
7) Pulp the cranberries and then mix stevia to it.
8) Pour the sauce over a strainer and transfer it to a bowl.
9) Mix xanthum gum and orange extract to the juice and stir until slightly thickened.
10) Spoon the glaze over the duck and roast for 10 to 13 minutes at 425 ° F / 218 ° C or until the skin is crispy.
11) Allow it to cool and serve it along with the remaining sauce.

Tip: If you prefer a spicy kick, you can add one jalapeno.

Nutritional Information:
➢ Calories: 393Kcal
➢ Fat: 32g
➢ Carbohydrates: 2g

➢ Proteins: 22g

25.   Chicken Avocado Casserole

The favour of the ripe creamy avocadoes along with creamy and tangy sour cream flavoured chicken is unbeatable and the hot sauce gives an extra boost of flavour.

Preparation Time: 15 Minutes

Cooking Time: 20 Minutes

Servings: 6

Ingredients:

- 8 Chicken Thighs, boneless and cooked
- 1 Onion, medium and thinly sliced
- 8-ounce Sour Cream
- 4 Avocados, small and sliced into thin strips
- 1 Red Hot
- 1 Pepper, medium and sliced into thin strips

- 8-ounce Cheddar Cheese
- Sea Salt and White Pepper, to taste

Method of Preparation:
1) Preheat the oven to 350 ° F / 175 ° C.
2) Place the thinly sliced avocado pieces on the greased baking pan.
3) Next, cook onion and pepper in a saucepan over medium heat or until transparent.
4) Now combine all the remaining ingredients in a large sized mixing bowl.
5) Spoon this chicken mixture onto the baking pan and spread it over.
6) Bake it in the oven for 17 minutes or until golden in colour.
7) Serve and enjoy.

Tip: To get a slightly herby flavoured, you may add dried basil along.

Nutritional Information:
- Calories: 549Kcal
- Fat: 40g
- Carbohydrates: 13g
- Proteins: 38g

26.   Malibu Chicken

Indulge yourself in this moist pork rind cheese crusted chicken tenders, and you will find yourself in heaven.

Preparation Time: 10 Minutes

Cooking Time: 40 Minutes

Servings: 4

Ingredients:

- 6 × 4 Chicken Breasts, cleaned and pat dried
- Sea Salt and White Pepper, to taste

To make the Malibu Dipping Sauce:

- ½ cup Mayonnaise
- 1 tablespoon Swerve
- 3 tablespoons Yellow Mustard

To make the Crumb Topping:

- ¾ cup crushed Pork Rinds
- 1 teaspoon granulated Onion
- ¾ cup Parmesan Cheese, grated
- 2 teaspoons Garlic, minced
- 1/8 teaspoon Pepper
- ¼ teaspoon Salt
- To Garnish:
- 8 pieces of Deli Ham, torn
- 4 slices of Swiss Cheese, grated

Method of Preparation:

1) Preheat the oven to 350 ° F / 175 ° C.
2) After that, place the pork rinds in a food processor and crush them into a nice grounded mixture.
3) Marinate the chicken with salt and pepper. Set it aside for half an hour.
4) Combine the Splenda, mayonnaise and yellow mustard in a small bowl until just combined.
5) Now, apply a quarter portion of the marinade over the chicken.
6) Marinate the chicken pieces for one hour.
7) Combine the pork rinds, parmesan cheese, garlic and onion in another bowl.
8) Spoon half the quantity of the pork rind mixture over the baking sheet.

9) Then, immerse the chicken pieces in the remaining pork rind mixture.

10) Bake the chicken pieces for 35 minutes or until the chicken is cooked.

11) Finally, garnish it with the ham and cheese and bake it for another five minutes or so.

Tip: This is a great make a day ahead meal.

Nutritional Information:

➢ Calories: 464Kcal

➢ Fat: 55g

➢ Carbohydrates: 4g

➢ Proteins: 46g

27.   Strawberry Turkey Burgers

Spice up your weekend meals with this super flavorful turkey burgers, which is an interesting combination of juicy berries, aromatic herbs, salty bacon and grounded turkey.

Preparation Time: 10 Minutes

Cooking Time: 30 Minutes

Servings: 4

Ingredients:

- 2 pounds Turkey, grounded
- 1 Egg, medium and farm raised
- 2 tablespoons Oregano, fresh and minced
- 1 strip Bacon, minced and cooked
- ½ teaspoons White Pepper
- 5 Strawberries, large and diced

- ½ cups Coconut Flour
- 2 tablespoons Olive Oil
- 3 cloves of Garlic, finely minced
- 1 ½ teaspoons Sea Salt

Method of Preparation:

1) Start by placing strawberries, oregano, bacon and garlic in a large mixing bowl and give a good toss.
2) To this, add the turkey, olive oil and seasoning and mix until everything is well combined.
3) Make patties out of this mixture and set it aside.
4) Take coconut flour in a plate and immerse the patties in it until they are coated.
5) Now, heat a wide skillet over medium heat and once hot, spoon in a teaspoon of oil.
6) Place the patties on the skillet and cook them for four minutes per side and flip and cook again for another four to five minutes.
7) Serve them hot with green salad.

Tip: Instead of coconut flour, you can also use almond meal.

Nutritional Information:

➤ Calories: 520Kcal
➤ Fat: 35g
➤ Carbohydrates: 3g
➤ Proteins: 42g

Desserts

28.   Chocolate Chip Cookie Fat Bombs

You may feel this recipe is a dream as these fat bombs give you the same warm and chewy chocolate chip cookie taste and texture you were used to before starting keto.

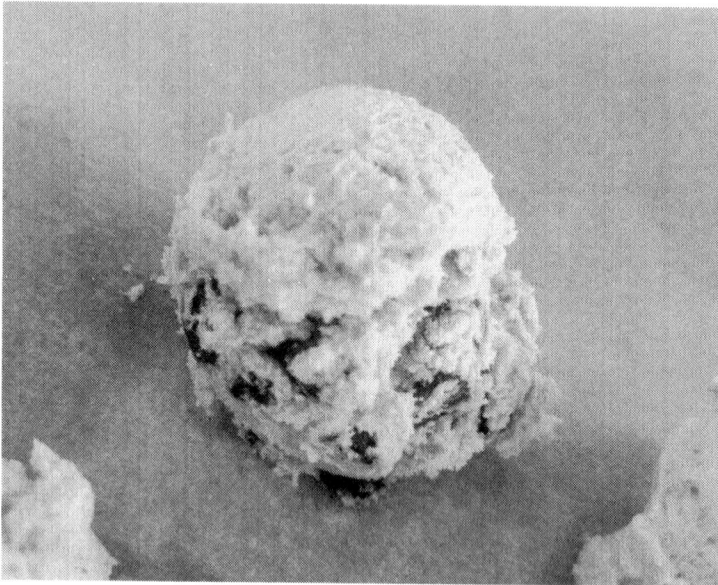

Preparation Time: 10 Minutes

Cooking Time: 25 Minutes

Servings: 4

Ingredients:

- 8 ounces Cream Cheese
- 4 ounces Baking Chips, sugar-free
- 1/3 cup Swerve Sweetener
- ½ cup Butter, organic
- 1 teaspoon Vanilla Extract

- ½ cup Nut butter

Method of Preparation:

1) Start by placing together all the ingredients in a large mixing bowl or until well combined.
2) Keep the dough in the refrigerator for about 20 to 25 minutes.
3) Grease an ice cream scoop and then scoop out the dough into a greased parchment paper.
4) Freeze again for another half hour or so and then serve immediately.

Tip: Adding a dash of salt can be a great idea.

Nutritional Information:

➤ Calories: 590Kcal
➤ Fat: 58g
➤ Carbohydrates: 7g
➤ Proteins: 12g

29.   Brown Butter Pecan Ice Cream

Can there be ice creams that are good for you? This beautifully flavoured caramelised ice cream with the nutty texture is one such one.

Preparation Time: 10 Minutes

Cooking Time: 20 Minutes

Servings: 3

Ingredients:

- 1 ½ cups Coconut Milk, unsweetened
- ¼ cup Pecans, crushed
- ¼ teaspoon xanthan gum
- ¼ cups Heavy Cream
- 25 drops Stevia, liquid
- 5 tablespoons Butter, organic and melted

Method of Preparation:

1) Heat butter in a wide saucepan over medium heat and to this; add pecans, stevia and heavy cream until well combined.

2) In another bowl, whisk together coconut milk and xanthan gum until mixed.

3) Combine the pecan mixture and coconut milk mixture together.

4) Transfer the mixture to an ice cream machine and follow the manufacturer's instruction.

Tip: If you prefer, adding a dash of salt can give a slightly different taste that is highly enjoyable.

Nutritional Information:

➢ Calories: 620Kcal
➢ Fat: 66g
➢ Carbohydrates: 4g
➢ Proteins: 10 g

30.   Chocolate Pudding

Want to satisfy your sugar craving while on keto? Then this chocolate pudding made with tofu is ideal as it is low in carb while being high in proteins and fat.

Preparation Time: 10 Minutes

Cooking Time: 20 Minutes

Servings: 1

Ingredients:

- 2 ½ ounce Tofu, firm
- 3 drops Vanilla Extract
- 2 teaspoon Coconut Oil
- ½ teaspoon natural Sweetener

- 1 tablespoon Canola Oil
- 2 teaspoon Chocolate Syrup
- 1 ½ teaspoon Baking Chocolate, unsweetened

Method of Preparation:

1) Heat the melting chocolate in a pan over low heat.
2) To this, add the coconut and canola oil and mix them well.
3) Place the chocolate oil mixture, sweetener, syrup and tofu into a food processor and blend until it becomes a smooth mixture.
4) Store in the refrigerator and serve when needed.

Tip: To enhance the taste, you can try adding berries or salted peanuts.

Nutritional Information:

- Calories: 380Kcal
- Fat: 31g
- Carbohydrates: 12g
- Proteins: 12g

31.   Raspberry in White Chocolate Cups

These desserts styled cups are creamy, sweet and utterly mouth – watering.

Preparation Time: 10 Minutes

Cooking Time: 40 Minutes

Servings: Make 12

Ingredients:

- ➢ ½ cups Cacao Butter, organic
- ➢ 1 teaspoon Vanilla Extract
- ➢ ½ cups Coconut Butter
- ➢ 3 tablespoons Swerve Sweetener
- ➢ 4 tablespoons Whey Powder
- ➢ ¼ cups Raspberries, crushed & freeze-dried

Method of Preparation:

1) Melt cacao and coconut butter using a double boiler and combine them well.
2) To this, spoon in the vanilla extract and mix.
3) In a bowl, stir in whey powder and sweetener.
4) Now, gradually spoon the whey sweetener mix to the butter mixture until they are well incorporated.
5) Finally, add the crushed raspberries and mix them again.
6) Transfer the batter into the muffin tins and place them in the refrigerator for at least 40 to 50 minutes or until set.

Tip: For a slightly different taste, you can try adding lemon extract.

Nutritional Information:
➤ Calories: 158Kcal
➤ Fat: 15.5g
➤ Carbohydrates: 1g
➤ Proteins: 2.6g

32.   Strawberry Chia Pudding

Would you like to make a pudding that is great as an afternoon snack that keeps you fill this dinner? Then this strawberry flavoured chia pudding would be an ideal choice.

Preparation Time: 10 Minutes

Cooking Time: 40 Minutes

Servings: 4

Ingredients:

- ½ cup whole Chia Seeds
- ½ cup Water
- 1 cup fresh Strawberries
- 1 cup Coconut Milk

- 3 tsp Vanilla Extract, unsweetened

Method of Preparation:

1) To begin with, combine coconut milk, strawberries and water in a blender and blend until it becomes a smooth paste.
2) Mix the coconut milk mixture with chia seeds and vanilla extract until combined.
3) Allow it to sit for overnight or a minimum of 45 minutes in the refrigerator.
4) Serve.

Tip: If you prefer a slightly tangy flavour, you can add a bit of lime zest.

Nutritional Information:

➤ Calories: 223Kcal
➤ Fat: 18.2g
➤ Carbohydrates: 12g
➤ Proteins: 5.5g

Wraps & Rolls

33.　　Spicy Pulled Pork Lettuce Wraps

Are you searching for a comfort food without guilt? Then these pulled pork wraps with their spicy and zesty taste and flavour are sure to please everyone.

Preparation Time: 10 Minutes

Cooking Time:

Servings: 3

- I5 Pork Loin Ribs, cooked and sliced
- 2 teaspoon Chilli Garlic Paste
- 1/3 Yellow Bell Pepper, sliced into thin strips
- ½ teaspoon Red Pepper Flake
- ¼ of 1 Onion, large and sliced into thin strips
- 6 pieces of Butter Lettuce

Method of Preparation:

1) Place each of the lettuce on a wide plate and fill each of them first with the meat, then with the bell pepper and finally with the onion.
2) Spoon the sauce of your choice over it.
3) Now, roll the lettuce into wraps and garnish it with the pepper flakes and chilli paste.

Tip: To enhance the flavour, you can try adding sour cream.

Nutritional Information:
➤ Calories: 338Kcal
➤ Fat: 25.6g
➤ Carbohydrates: 2.4g
➤ Proteins: 22.7g

34.　Smoked Salmon and Avocado Wraps

Simple and straight forward, these vibrantly coloured well-seasoned wraps celebrate the sweet creaminess of avocado and richness of salmon. Try it once!

Preparation Time: 10 Minutes

Cooking Time: 30 Minutes

Servings: 4

Ingredients:

To make the Wraps:

- 3 Eggs, medium and farm raised
- 1 teaspoon Celtic Sea Salt
- ¼ cup Coconut Flour, organic
- 1 tablespoon Extra-Virgin Olive Oil
- ½ cup Sour Cream
- Coconut Oil, as needed

To make the avocado spread:

- 1 Avocado
- 1 tablespoon Chives, chopped finely
- 1 tablespoon extra-virgin Olive Oil
- ½ cup Sour Cream
- ¼ teaspoon Celtic Sea Salt
- 1 tablespoon Lemon juice

To make the Filling:

- 4 ounces smoked Salmon
- Fresh Chives, chopped
- 4 ounces Crab Meat
- Lemon zest, as needed

Method of Preparation:

1) Combine all the ingredients needed to make the wrap in a blender or processor and blend until it becomes a smooth mixture.
2) Heat a wide skillet over medium heat.
3) Spoon a bit of coconut oil over the skillet and scoop ¼ portion of the batter into the skillet.
4) Spread it out with the back of the ladle until it becomes a round shape.
5) Cook for one minute or until it is lightly browned.
6) Now flip it over cook for further one minute.

7) Repeat the procedure with the remaining batter and keep all the wraps, one each, between two layers of tissue paper and place it in the refrigerator.

8) To make the spread, mix all the ingredients needed for the spread in the processor and blend until it becomes a smooth paste.

9) Transfer it to a bowl and set it aside.

10) Finally, take the wraps one by one and then spread the avocado mix and then top it with the smoked salmon and crab on top.

11) Roll the wrap tightly and then garnish it with the chives and lemon zest.

12) Serve it along with a green salad.

Tip: If you prefer, you can very little amount of grated carrot also.

Nutritional Information:
➤ Calories: 282Kcal
➤ Fat: 25g
➤ Carbohydrates: 1.5g
➤ Proteins: 9.35g

35.   Zucchini Rolls with Goat Cheese

Zucchini and goat cheese wraps is a brightly flavoured, vibrant and easy appetiser that is sure to hook you to its taste and texture.

Preparation Time: 10 Minutes

Cooking Time: 15 Minutes

Servings: 6

Ingredients:

- 1 Zucchini, washed and ends trimmed off
- 1 teaspoon Dill, dried
- 6-ounce Goat Cheese, soft
- Sea Salt, as needed
- 1 teaspoon Mint, dried
- White Pepper, as needed
- Oil, as needed

Method of Preparation:

1) Slice the zucchini into small slices using a mandoline.

2) Combine pepper, salt and olive oil in another bowl and then apply it over the zucchini slices.

3) Grill the zucchini at medium heat for two to three sides per minute or until browned.

4) In the meantime, mix goat cheese, mint and dill together in another bowl.

5) Divide them equally and make cylinder shapes out of it.

6) Place these shapes inside a zucchini and roll it tightly and press it with a toothpick.

Tip: Serve it along with a green salad for a complete meal.

Nutritional Information:

➢ Calories: 186Kcal
➢ Fat: 14g
➢ Carbohydrates: 2g
➢ Proteins: 13g

36. Chicken Salad Wraps

A simple chicken salad recipe flavoured with garlic powder, parsley and mayonnaise and which is that tasty and brilliantly simple.

Preparation Time: 10 Minutes

Cooking Time: 40 Minutes

Servings: 5

Ingredients:

- 1-pound Chicken Thighs, boneless
- ½ cup Mayonnaise, homemade
- ½ teaspoon Sea Salt
- 1 cup Celery, diced
- 10 leaves baby leaf Lettuce
- ½ teaspoon Pepper
- ¼ teaspoon Garlic powder
- 1 tablespoon Parsley, chopped finely

- 1 tablespoon Olive Oil

Method of Preparation:

1) Preheat the oven to 390 ° F / 180 ° C.
2) Season the chicken with salt, olive oil, garlic powder and pepper. Set it aside for 10 to 15 minutes.
3) Arrange the chicken pieces on a greased baking sheet and roast it for about 25 minutes or until cooked.
4) Allow it to cool for some time and dice it into small pieces.
5) In the meantime, toss together mayonnaise, parsley and celery together in another bowl until combined.
6) Finally, add the chicken pieces into this and give another good toss.
7) Spoon this chicken mixture over the lettuce leaves and serve.

Tip: For a more crunchiness, you can add pecans.

Nutritional Information:
- Calories: 320Kcal
- Fat: 24g
- Carbohydrates: 7g
- Proteins: 16g

37.   Low carb Egg Salad

This is a high-fat simple egg salad that is perfect for weekday meals. You just can't beat the flavours of homemade mayonnaise mixed with egg.

Preparation Time: 10 Minutes

Cooking Time: 20 Minutes

Servings: 4

Ingredients:

- 6 Eggs, large and farm raised, hard boiled
- 1 teaspoon Lemon juice
- Kosher Salt, as needed
- 2 tablespoons Mayonnaise, preferably homemade
- ¼ teaspoons Sea Salt
- 1 teaspoon Dijon Mustard
- White Pepper, as needed

- Lettuce leaves, if needed

Method of Preparation:

1) To start with, halve the hard boiled eggs and place them in the food processor and pulse them until it becomes a smooth paste.
2) Next, stir in the mayonnaise, mustard, lemon juice, salt and pepper and pulse it again.
3) Transfer the mixture into a bowl.
4) Take the lettuce leaves and place the egg filling inside.
5) Roll it tightly and hold it with a toothpick.

Tip: If desired, you can roll the lettuce wraps with bacon.

Nutritional Information:

➢ Calories: 150Kcal
➢ Fat: 10g
➢ Carbohydrates: 3g
➢ Proteins: 9g

Substitution

Substitution for Egg

One good substitution for egg is flax seeds. This substitution works particularly well in baked goods. For this mix one tablespoon of flax seeds with three tablespoon of water until it is fully absorbed. This can be used instead of one egg.

Substitution for Diary Milk

They are many good substitutes for diary milk like soy milk, hemp milk, rice milk, almond milk etc.

Substitution for Cheese

Nutritional yeast flakes are good substitutions for cheese.

Recipe for Homemade Low Carb Mayonnaise

Preparation Time: 5 Minutes

Cooking Time: 15 Minutes

Ingredients:

- 1 Egg, large and farm raised
- 1 cup Olive Oil, light
- 1 tablespoon Apple Cider Vinegar
- Salt and Pepper, as needed

Method of Preparation:

1) Place the egg, salt and pepper in a tall container and whisk it lightly using a blender.
2) To this gradually add the olive oil and continue whisking in low speed until it becomes a thick sauce.
3) Add the vinegar and mix it again. If it becomes too thick, add more oil.
4) You can add your choice of seasoning like herbs, lemon juice etc. to make seasoned mayonnaise.

Homemade Recipe for Low Carb Marinara Sauce

Preparation Time: 10 Minutes

Cooking Time: 5 Minutes

Ingredients:

- 28 oz can San Marzano Tomatoes, peeled
- 1 teaspoon Parsley, dried
- ¼ teaspoon Black Pepper
- 1 teaspoon Basil, dried
- ½ teaspoon Red Pepper Flakes
- ¼ cup Extra Virgin Olive Oil
- 1 teaspoon Onion powder
- 2 tablespoon Red Wine Vinegar
- 1 teaspoon Garlic powder
- 1 teaspoon Oregano, dried
- 1 teaspoon Salt

Method of Preparation:
1) To start with, place the tomatoes in a blender and puree it.
2) Next, add all the remaining ingredients in it and blend it again until it becomes a smooth paste.

Conclusion

Once you have started off with ketogenic diet, you are sure to see lots of benefits accruing. The fact that you have control and a strong will over your eating habits is one significant advantage. And if you were addicted to taking food all day then you might have noticed that ketogenic diet is more filling and that you are not always under hunger pangs and your appetite is more balanced now. So make sure that you go forward with the ketogenic diet and enjoy a healthy life.

Copyright 2017 by The International BookSCA Company - All rights reserved.

All rights Reserved. No part of this publication or the information in it may be quoted from or reproduced in any form by means such as printing, scanning, photocopying or otherwise without prior written permission of the copyright holder.

Disclaimer and Terms of Use: Effort has been made to ensure that the information in this book is accurate and complete, however, the author and the publisher do not warrant the accuracy of the information, text and graphics contained within the book due to the rapidly changing nature of science, research, known and unknown facts and internet. The Author and the publisher do not hold any responsibility for errors, omissions or contrary interpretation of the subject matter herein. This book is presented solely for motivational and informational purposes only.

23616076R00057

Printed in Great Britain
by Amazon